MY GRANDCHILD AND I

A Visit to New Orleans

Suzanne Wallace

Copyright © 2019 by Suzanne Wallace. 794082

ISBN: Softcover   978-1-7960-2435-7
       Hardcover   978-1-7960-2436-4
       EBook   978-1-7960-2434-0

Print information available on the last page

Rev. date: 03/28/2019

To order additional copies of this book, contact:
Xlibris
1-888-795-4274
www.Xlibris.com
Orders@Xlibris.com

MY
GRANDCHILD
AND I

A Visit to New Orleans

My grandchild and I
Have many things to do,

We are going to the museum

And then to the Zoo.

We will ride a streetcar,
Yes, we will do that too.

My grandchild and I
Have many things to do,

We will get some costumes
And watch a parade,

We will eat po-boys

And sit in the shade.

We will visit the library
And a book we will choose,

We will take long walks

And an occasional snooze.

We will visit the Aquarium
And admire the fish,

We will dine in a restaurant
On a good Cajun dish.

We will go to the Cathedral
Then sit in a Jackson Square,

We will watch the artists
And have our portraits down there.

We will each have a snowball,

And ride along the lake.

And everywhere we go,
Our pictures we will take.

We will ride on a riverboat
And hear the Calliope play.

We will go on a swamp tour
On another day.

We will get umbrellas
And second line,

We will have coffee, milk and beignets,
Now, that's just fine.

My grandchild and I have
many things to do.

The plans are getting bolder and bolder,

But we may have to wait
To carry them out,

At least 'til she's a little older!

The End

No!

It is just the beginning.